My Cat and I

Written by

J.N. Wynn

For my Luna,

Always my Inspurrration

For permission requests, please contact:
J.N. Wynn

Email: ourlittlemoon@outlook.com

ISBN Hardcover: 979-8-9936147-1-7
ISBN Hardcover: 9798272963826
ISBN Hardcover: 9798260350430
ISBN Paperback: 979-8-9936147-2-4
ISBN Paperback: 9798272879233
ISBN Paperback: 9798260351604

Cover and interior design by: J.N. Wynn
Printed in the United States of America
This is a work of creative inspurrration. Any resemblance to real events or individuals, living or deceased, is purely coincidental.

Made with love, purrs, and a little bit of sunshine.

A book is the soul of the author's spirit.

Hi, Cat.

Hi, Girl.

Cat, life is
hard.

If it wasn't, how would we know
we're living? That's a part of
purring.

Cat, teach me the
meaning of life

The meaning of life isn't something that can be taught. It's something you learn along the way. One paw at a time.

Cat, why do life give and take?

We cannot control
what we are given.
Sometimes life decides
for us.

Life takes to teach, and gives
to keep us going.

That's why I have nine lives.

Cat, maybe I've tried too hard.
Maybe what I should be doing is
simply letting things be

Maybe you don't need to stop trying.
Maybe you just need to stop fighting yourself.

Even a cat knows when to stop chasing shadows.

There is nothing wrong
with trying.
It means we haven't
given up.

Maybe I'm just too
kind.

There is nothing wrong with
being kind.
Sometimes we forget that
kindness is a virtue, as much as
pautience.

Kindness is not a weakness.
Meow it with me.
Kindness is not a weakness.

Cat, why do people hurt each other?

Sometimes we see enemies in
others,
but we don't see that we are
our own worst enemies.

We hiss at the shadows, never
realizing they're our own.

Be kind to yourself.

Even when you think
you don't deserve a
purr

Forgiveness is the silence
we've long forgotten.

Cat, sometimes grief makes me
sad.

Maybe sadness can be a
kind of strength.

It teaches us to treasure the

warm, cuddly moments even

more

Cat, what is the meaning of
being human

Maybe it's to feel everything,
even things that make us sad

Sometimes being human can feel heavy inside.

Sometimes silence speaks louder than words.

But even in the hardest times, it helps us see how strong we truly are.

Don't give up.

Keep chasing the light.

Happiness isn't something that's
always there.
It comes and goes, but it
always returns.
So does sadness.

Cat, what is one of the hardest
things in life?

Being honest with yourself

Cat, I'm afraid

Being afraid doesn't make you weak.

Even the strongest cats are
afraid of their own shadow.

Cat, is it wrong to seek help?

Seeking help is refusing to surrender.

Cat, is it wrong to be different!

Being different is okay too.
It means we are our own pawson

One of a paw kind, like every

pawprint

We all need a reason to keep purring.

Tell me, what is yours,
Girl?

Cat, what if I don't have a reason?

That's okay. Just being
here is a good enough
reason

Sometimes the things we need most are right in front of us.

We just need the courage
to see them

Cat, what if I dont have the courage?

It'll be okay.

I'll be right here until you find it.

Even the smallest step

forward is an achievement.

Cat, What is the best thing in the world!

Love.

The only thing worth purring for.

Girl, remember this.

One of the biggest lies in life is purrlieving that being purrfect is what makes you special.

You dont have to be
purrfect

to matter

Cat, isn't curiosity dangerous?

Only when you stop having it.
Keep learning, keep wondering.
that's how we grow.

Cat, why is life so difficult

Because the things that matter
never come easy.
If they did, we'd forget how
precious they are. The world is
only meowgical when we purr-
lieve in it.

Cat, can love fade?

Only when it's the wrong pawson.

Cat, sometimes people don't believe in me.

Then purr-lieve in yourself.

What if I can't.

You can.

You just have to purr-lieve.

All of the purr-tential is already inside of you.

Cat, sometimes I feel so alone.

Loneliness isn't so bad.
It helps you see who's
truly there.

Cat, I feel like my words are
lost.

Then let's go find
them.

Cat, why isn't tomorrow
guaranteed!

Because if it were, we wouldn't purr
what we have meow.

Cat, What if I fail?

Failures are a part of life. They help us learn.
There is no such thing as a failure.

Anything is pawsible, as long
as you keep dreaming.

Cat, what should I be when I grow up?

Be a dreamer.

Dreamers are the ones with a vision

And how do I do that?

Do the impawssible, and you'll never
battle doubt again.

Cat, what if the darkness chooses
to stay?

Then light a candle and hiss it away. The darkness is only scary if you hisstinate.

Cat, what if life feels overwhelming?

Just focus on what is in front of you.
One paw at a time.

The storm will pass.
You just have to keep on going. Be
your own meowtivation

Cat, what if the storm never goes away?

It will.

There is always a rainbow waiting on the other side.

All it takes is a little bit of purrtience until it meowmerges."

Remember...

Life is a long journey. It's
worth the wait.

Why?

Because it's the most beautiful adventure
of all

Cat, why don't Mommy and
Daddy love each other anymore?

Sometimes love changes shape.
It stops fitting the way it used
to.
That doesn't mean they love you
any less. They always love you
furrever.

Cat, what is the best part of me?

Being you.

And what is the best thing about you?

Knowing that I am enough.

Cat, why did life choose us?

Because we have so
much to offer.

And what if we don't?

Then we just haven't
found it yet.

Cat, what if our hearts are broken?

Then we just purr them back together, one piece at a time.

Cat, what is the silliest thing we do in life?

Compare our worth to what others think of us.

Cat, where is home?

Home is not a place,
but where we are
together.

Cat, how far can life take us?

As far as we want.

Sometimes we forget how much love the world still has to offer.

Cat, it's raining outside.

That's good.
Sometimes the world cries with us, so we
know we're not alone.

Cat, the sun is out again.

Isn't that life?
It rains on us,
then gives us sunshine right
after.

Cat, why do people ask us to smile?

Maybe because a smile
is a reminder that
there's still good in the
world.

Cat, why does sadness make our
hearts ache?

It's our heart reminding us
we're human.

It's okay to be sad.
Sadness is a part of life.
It's how we turn that sadness into
Inspurrration.
That is what makes it powerful.

Weakness isn't showing your emotions.

Weakness is hiding them.

Cat, someday it feels easier to just give up.

But if everything in life
came easy,
then what would be worth
purring for?

Cat, is it okay to laugh when you're hurting?

Joy doesn't mean you've forgotten the pain.

It means you've survived it.

Cat, sometimes I feel like
I'm the problem.

Maybe some problems just
take longer to understand.

Cat, We didn't do anything
today.

That's fine.

Maybe nothing is
exactly what we
needed.

Cat, why do people tell us to be strong, but never teach us that crying is also a kind of strength?

Because they forgot that
crying cleanses the
heart like rain cleans
the sky

Sometimes it's easy to forget we're only human."

Cat, why do people ask us to move on, when healing means staying long enough to understand why it hurts?

Because moving on is easier than staying. We hide when it hurts, but healing begins when we stop hiding.

Remembering what
we've forgotten
is part of finding who
we are.

Cat, but what if I don't remember?

Then look inside your heart . It will remind you.

Cat, what if I become
broken?

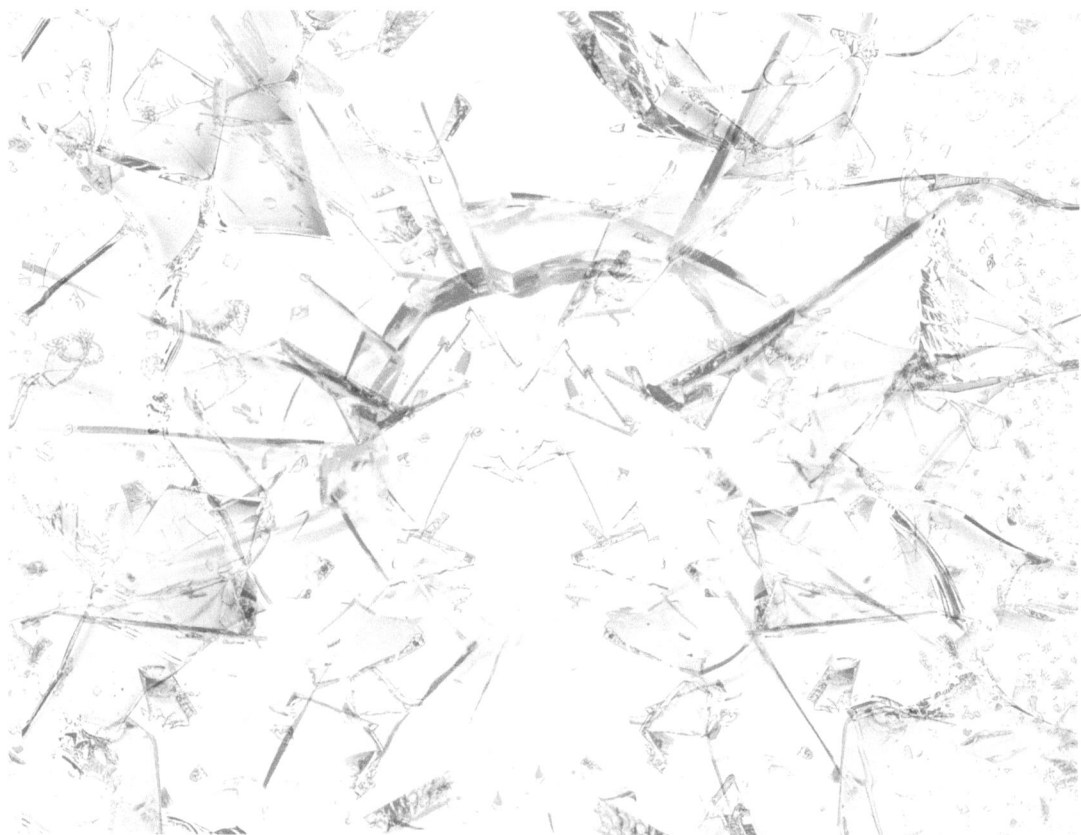

Then we'll pick up the pieces
together.
Even broken things can shine
when the light finds them.

Smile.

Smile.

It's okay to smile even when you're

sad.

Cat, what is the best
story?

The best story in life is your own.

Greatness is born from the challenges we face.

Cat, when someone leaves us,
are they gone furrever?

No. When someone leaves us, they're never truly gone. They become the pawprints we carry within our hearts.

I'm happy you're here, cat.

I'm happy you're here too, girl.

Cat, don't leave me.

I'll never.

The End

www.ingramcontent.com/pod-product-compliance
Lightning Source LLC
Chambersburg PA
CBHW041547260326
41914CB00016B/1581